ROW, ROW, ROW YOUR BOAT

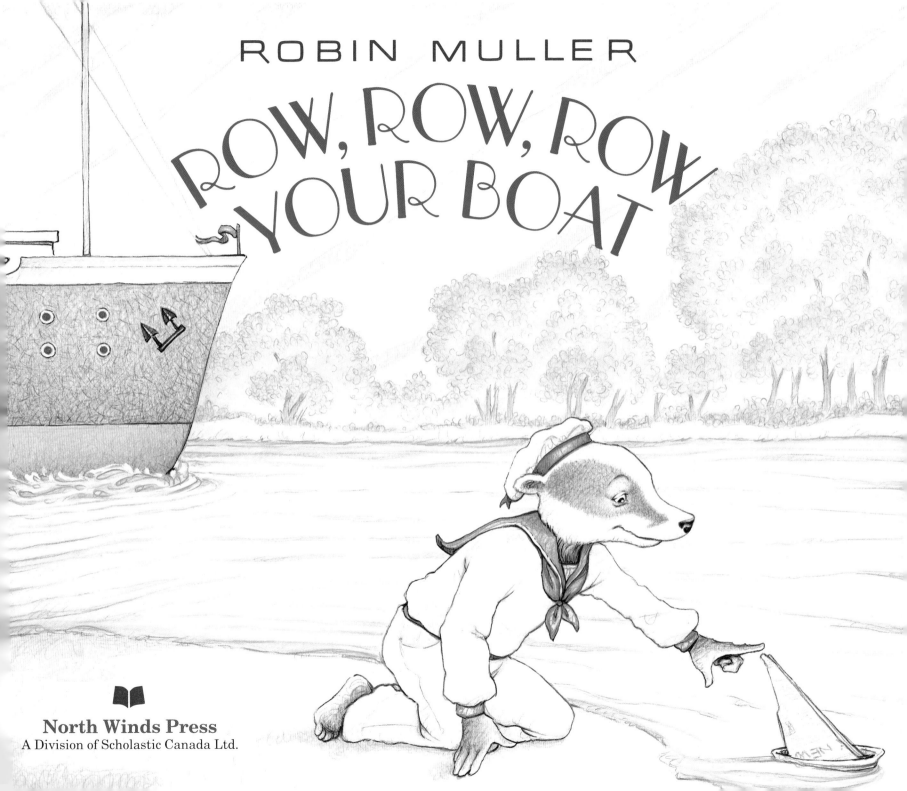

ROBIN MULLER

ROW, ROW, ROW YOUR BOAT

North Winds Press
A Division of Scholastic Canada Ltd.

To Katalin and Garrett McLean
and to their new little cousin — Lauren Lindsay Perkins

The illustrations for this book were drawn on bond paper with Laurentien coloured pencils.

6 5 4 3 2 1   Printed in Canada   3 4 5 6 7/9

Canadian Cataloguing in Publication Data

Muller, Robin.
    Row, row, row your boat

ISBN 0-590-74584-0

I. Title.

PS8576.U55R69   1993   jC813'.54   C92-095360-3
PZ7.M85Ro   1993

A badger, on a summer's day,
sat dreaming on the sand.
"A life at sea's the one for me,
so goodbye to the land!"

Row, row, row your boat,
gently down the stream,
merrily, merrily, merrily, merrily —
life is but a dream.

The other badgers laughed at him.
"Your fancies never last!
You'll be back here," he heard them jeer,
"before the day is past."

The badger didn't care at all.
His path was crystal clear.
"A sailor's free to sail the sea,
and travel far from here!"

Row, row, row your boat,
gently down the stream,
merrily, merrily, merrily, merrily —
life is but a dream.

A chimp was playing in a tree
and heard his rousing call.
"Let me come too, O Badger, do.
I am but very small."

The badger helped the chimp aboard.
"We two will sail the sea!
The boat is big – we'll dance a jig
and sing, just you and me."

Row, row, row your boat, gently down the stream,
merrily, merrily, merrily, merrily — life is but a dream.

A llama and a platypus
were fishing by the shore.
Their dangling lines became entwined,
and now the crew was four.

Row, row, row your boat, gently down the stream,
merrily, merrily, merrily, merrily — life is but a dream.

A hippo watching from the bank
was laughing at their plight.
Her joy soon passed as down she splashed
into the foam so white.

Row, row, row your boat,
gently down the stream,
merrily, merrily, merrily, merrily —
life is but a dream.

A crocodile, so mean and vile,
then spied the noisy bunch.
"This crew," thought he, "my meal will be,"
and rang the bell for lunch.

And from the shore this loathsome croc,
his jaws so fierce and long,
began to float toward the boat . . .

. . . but then he heard the song.

Row, row, row your boat,
gently down the stream,
merrily, merrily, merrily, merrily —
life is but a dream.

An ostrich, moose and porcupine
were splashing in the foam.
This soggy horde then climbed aboard,
the seven seas to roam.

The animals all crowded in,
till room there wasn't any.
The badger's dream had fled, it seemed —
the boat had one too many.

The weary badger said goodbye,
and waved them out to sea.
"A sailor's life has too much strife . . ."

". . . A train's the thing for me!"

I've been working on the railroad
all the live-long day.
I've been
working
on the
railroad . . .